The Absence of Mind
A Memoir of Mental Illness
By Maeve McCrea

While every precaution has been taken in the preparation of this book, the publisher assumes no responsibility for errors or omissions, or for damages resulting from the use of the information contained herein.

THE ABSENCE OF MIND

First edition. April 1, 2023.

Copyright © 2023 Maeve McCrea.

ISBN: 979-8215859520

Written by Maeve McCrea.

Acknowledgments

This book would not have been possible if not for the constant encouragement and love from my family. After my second hospitalization I told my mother about how I had been writing this book to cope with my depression and anxiety. Hearing her say that she thought I had a way with words, it only made me want to write more. Christian, thank you for your love. For being an ear to listen and always offering to be an editor when needed. Thank you for being a therapist when even words couldn't save me. Thank you to my medication manager Ashleigh Brown, your belief that I could get better as long as I kept trying. You were the first doctor that believed in me. Finally, to my therapist Mari Rhodes, thank you for always being there, even at the times I have run away. You always know just what to say and to help me fight my over-thinking. Thank you for your kindness and support.

Foreword

The book you are about to read is a look into my life. Told through diary entries and poetry. These weren't just words that came to mind, writing became a coping mechanism that I had to use to let out the frustrations and pain that I felt. The struggles throughout the years have been overwhelming for me, writing out my thoughts helped me to better understand myself. I must warn you that the words you are about to read may not be easy for some. These writings deal with themes of childhood sexual abuse and rape, adulthood sexual assault, graphic self-mutilation, mental disorders, along with suicidal attempts and ideations. Please do not use my words as a manual to hurt yourself, I pray and hope that this book can help you to be able to express the feelings you have. To know that you aren't alone. To help you to be honest with yourself as I have tried to be with myself. If you or anyone you know may be struggling with issues that are along these themes, I have included some phone numbers below that I know firsthand have helped me many times. Share these numbers and keep them for yourself. Try to stay healthy. You are loved. There is always someone that wants to hear you and help you. In this book you will watch me fall and rise. Growth is a continuous effort in life. There is always a glimmer of hope. I wish you happiness. Also, the names of people and places in this book have been changed to respect the privacy of everyone involved. Thank you.

US National Suicide Prevention Hot Line/Text Line

988

Crisis Text Line

Text Connect to 741741

RAINN National Sexual Assault Hotline

1-800-656-4673

01/03/19

Cain and I have talked about having a polyamorous relationship in the past. At first when he mentioned it, I was really against it. I mean we have been together for almost eight years now. Aren't I enough? He brought it up again a few days ago, talking about how he wants to explore different kinds of relationships beside ours, that he wants to experience emotional love different from mine. I cautiously said we should give it a try. I guess it wouldn't be so bad to date other people. He explained it saying imagine dating someone for a long time but they don't meet all of your emotional needs. With being polyamorous you can be with multiple people that way all of your emotional/physical needs can be met.

Cain wants us to both join dating apps so that we can find someone we both deem okay for each other. Thing is, I have a friend who already practices polyamory with their wife. Jeremy and I have been close for years, he's one of my best friends. I asked Cain if I could go for Jeremy instead of searching out a stranger online. He got jealous pretty quickly saying he was hoping we could find partners online together. Maybe he wanted to pick a person for me? I'm not sure. I think it would be perfect with Jeremy though, we have the same work schedule and have all the same likes. But I can see how jealous Cain is of it all working out so quickly for me with already knowing someone. Then like an hour after that conversation Cain came back up to me and said I should give it a go with Jeremy, to see how I like polyamory.

So, Jeremy and I have been texting all day. He asked his wife if it was cool that he and I try having a first date, just to see if the vibes are there. She was chill with the idea. He and I flirted a little and I mean it isn't the worst thing. Jeremy is cute and he's really funny. We've been sharing dumb but sexual memes the past few hours. This first date actually sounds kind of fun.

01/04/2019

Well Cain hasn't talked to me at all today. I guess that jealousy thing is happening again. I went up to him and said that I will just cancel on things with Jeremy. It isn't worth messing up my relationship with Cain if he doesn't accept who I am dating. It sucks a bit; Jeremy and I texted all yesterday and then talked all night at work together. I had butterflies in my stomach when I drove home this morning. I guess fuck it.

Later today I started talking to this guy instead that I met on this relationship anarchy Facebook page that Cain recommended I research. His name is Alastor. He's pretty cute and has a serious kind of personality. Alastor says he is looking to be in a dominant/submissive relationship. That is definitely different from how my relationship with Cain is, but it is something that has interested me. It's not like I've never heard of such a thing before. Cain and I have explored it in the bedroom, but it would be different for it to actually be what the relationship is based on. Alastor and I talked on and off all day. He lives a few states away but we've talked about hopefully meeting up someday soon. He seems so eager to meet eventually. We shall see how everything continues to go.

01/07/19

Things are going okay; they've turned a bit interesting. Alastor, I found out has another girlfriend he has been with and he has asked if I want to be in a three-person relationship with them both. I guess I am going for super polyamory over here. She seems nice, her name is Cecilia. When we were talking last night, he told me to talk to her and then he hung up the phone so it was just she and I. He calls her his kitten. I told her how much I love cats too so we've been bonding over that.

Later on in the night I talked with Alastor about my conversation with Cecilia and he got upset with me over the whole she is his kitten so I can't have the same pet name. It was petty to be upset over and he spent like an hour or two yelling at me through video calls and angry text messages. He said that in a dom/sub relationship I am supposed to listen to everything my dom says. I mean we are barely in a relationship and this dom/sub thing is new to me. I've never had a hierarchy thing going in my relationships. I'm definitely not one to like being told what to do I don't think. He "punished" me for upsetting him by making me write sentences for him. Seems dumb but I did it anyway. I didn't write the sentence he wanted me to write, I was petty back and wrote whatever I wanted.

01/08/19

Alastor yelled and cursed at me on the phone about my sentences, he made me start writing them over again but then I just burst out crying because I got overwhelmed and he hung up the phone on me. He said how I must not really want this dom/sub relationship if I won't follow his rules. We just started talking, I don't know. I'm just not used to this. He even told me he loves me and that I've made him fall for me. That I am putting all this pressure on him but also tempting him constantly. This is all happening so fast. I've literally just started talking to him what a few days ago? He's angrily telling me he loves me? None of this seems right. It's just overwhelming and giving me anxiety. He calls me fifty times a day and if I don't answer he gets pissed at me. I'm an overnight employee, I sleep during the day. He always seems to be mad at me.

01/15/19

I texted Alastor and Cecilia, I told them how this is all moving so fast and how I don't know if this is right for me. How uncomfortable this relationship feels. They said it was fine and that they figured me being new at this they understood if it wasn't for me. A minute later though Alastor private messaged me and called me names. He said I was just stringing him along the whole time to hurt him. I apologized; I mean that isn't what I intended to happen at all. I don't even want to be polyamorous but I feel like I have to because it is what Cain wants.

It all feels wrong. This is all too much and it is freaking me out. These angry insulting conversations are not how I want a relationship. Alastor texting me demanding my attention all day. He would call me when I was trying to work. None of this is healthy. I mean he sounds so angry. He has an idea of where I work. I don't know… He's talked before about fights he has been in and that he has anger issues. This all just has me scared. I told Cain about me being scared. He said how I shouldn't have told someone about so much in my life so soon. But I thought I was starting a relationship with this guy, and you have to be honest for a relationship to work right? Again, I didn't even want this polyamory thing in the first place!

I've blocked all communications with Alastor. But it doesn't help me feel any safer. I'm honestly terrified from how Alastor sounded. What if he shows up to my work? What if he tries to hurt me? God, I haven't had a panic attack in years, but all of these overwhelming emotions are stirring up. It feels hot and I like I can't breathe. Why did Cain want to try polyamory in the first place? We've been together for eight years, I thought we were fine. In the hotel we stayed at after the house fire last year when I asked him why he wants polyamory he told me it was because he wanted to "experience emotional love from other people". Does that mean I am not enough for him anymore? We have been through so much together. Why does anything have to change? Then he sat there and tried explaining "relationship anarchy" to me. That just sounds like people who don't want to use labels. But Cain and I have been engaged for eight years. We chose our labels. Does he not want to be engaged anymore? Does he not love me anymore?

01/17/2019

Cain hasn't let it go that I even considered Jeremy. He got upset with me again but also said I should give it another go with him? That this Alastor thing was my fault and yet it would be a safer bet if I went with someone I already know. I am too confused. Whatever, I gave it a shot with Jeremy again. I feel bad going back and forth on him. When I asked Jeremy that we give it a go again he got a little anxious sounding but said yes. So, we flirted again. Then hours later Cain freaked out on me again saying how I only wanna be with Jeremy because I want to leave him. What? You're the one that told me to go back to Jeremy! Now I am confused with all of my feelings. I love Cain with all of my heart, but I have flirted with Jeremy twice now and I'm not gonna lie that is giving me some feelings too. Jeremy has been my best friend for years now, suddenly finding myself attracted to him has me really lost. Then I also still feel unsafe because of Alastor. I've literally been having panic attacks when I am alone and while I am at work. Doesn't help either that a night ago there was a peeping tom outside of my bedroom looking in on me while I was lying comfortably half dressed on the bed playing with my phone and texting Jeremy while he was at work. The guy talked through the window at me saying "Yeah big girl, take it off for me". I pretended not to hear him and I called the cops but there wasn't much that could be done. I mean I have worked retail for years; I've had lots of sexual harassment and stalking thrown at me more times than I could count. But someone outside my window ?? Alastor having been aggressive to me? Cain angry at me all of the time? I can't take this.

Cheating? Polyamory? Jeremy 01/18/19

I feel so raw and exposed
Like I am bleeding without a cut
I've started self-harming
I haven't done this in years
Is this what it feels to be alive?
I don't even know if I understand how being alive feels
My emotions leave me nauseous
My confusion about why I felt this way in the first place
What made me notice Jeremy at all?
I have comfort, safety, and happiness at home with Cain
Yet still my eyes looked at Jeremy in curiosity
I feel like I broke everything I have
The trust and bond is shaken
I thought about what it would be like to sleep with another man
I thought about him touching me and if it would make me feel good
My imagination ran wild
My fiancé asking me if I am so unhappy with him that these thoughts
manifested
But that isn't it
I don't know what it is
I feel selfish
I feel sick
He asks did I want some kind of adventure to feel alive
I don't know
He asks if I am unhappy with him
No no that isn't it
I love you
I cannot imagine a moment without you
That is the most frightening thought that could ever come
You told me it was okay

I don't know why you started any of this
The thought frightens me that maybe this is some sort of religious
struggle for me to climb through
That I haven't been faithful enough in my religion and temptations
outside of my relationship have found its way to me
I don't fucking know
I want to cry
I want to lay in a ball and weep over nothing
Dammit
I don't know what I want
I am selfish
I just want happiness within myself
I want to feel at peace
I'm sorry

Nausea

01/16/19 - Nothing to eat

01/17/19 - Protein Bar

01/18/19 - Protein Bar, 2 bananas

01/19/19 - 2 Bananas, handful of peanuts

01/20/19 - Deli lunchable

01/21/19 – 5 Carrot sticks, yogurt cup, fruit cup

01/22/19 – 2 Bagels with cream cheese, whopper with small fries

01/23/19 – Three bowls at Mongolian restaurant with plate of rice

01/24/19 – Nothing to eat

01/25/19 – Deli lunchable, yogurt cup

01/26/19 – 1 Banana, deli lunchable

01/27/19 – 2 Cheese sticks, deli lunchable < puked this all up, cream cheese with bagel chips

01/28/19 – Frozen chicken Parmesan meal, few bites of key lime pie

01/29/19 – Admittance into mental hospital

First Hospital Stay 01/21/19

It feels like there is acid in my throat
A rock on my chest
My heart wants to bleed through my eyes

First Hospital Stay 01/23/2019

Bandaged wounds cut open only to be sewn closed to heal again

13

First Hospital Stay. Spoken Words 01/25/2019

Every time I walk into my mother's house memories still flood back in
I walk into my old bedroom and stare at the ceiling fan
Counting it as it spins
One, two, three, four
Red, blue, green, yellow
I used to repeat the colors over and over
Maybe if I memorized them, maybe if I did well in school, maybe if I was kind to him then he wouldn't touch me
I would smile at his face, laugh along with my family
If I played along everything could be fine
If I was a good child then maybe he wouldn't climb on top of me anymore
If I was good then maybe I would feel connected and safe again
I was never good enough
But couldn't they see?
I listened so well, I liked mom's new boyfriend
I was so happy that he moved into my home
Isn't the fact that I am behaving enough to make him stop?
I told
I told my counselor at school
I was tired of telling the bus driver to continue passed my stop
I was tired of feeling used
I was tired of living up to my twelve year old self telling me that I wasn't good enough
I told
And I regretted it instantly
Everyone would know
Everyone did know

My sister blamed me for my mother's lost happiness
Why had I always been so kind to him if this really had happened?
My brother called me a whore saying how I wanted it, that I stole moms
boyfriend
My mother was angry at me
Why didn't I tell her?
Why had I kept this secret and then told the counselor?
She could have handled it
She could have fixed it
I didn't want her to know
I was ashamed
Was I wrong to be kind?
Was I to blame?
I was good
I did what I thought I was supposed to do
I told an adult
The police questioning and not believing me
Saying that a twelve year old is old enough to understand her body
maybe I had instigated it
You've masturbated before that must mean you have experimented
You've had a boyfriend that must mean you are experienced
Dammit, he was my first for everything
His eyes still haunt me as they stared hungrily at my face
I laid there frozen
Never moving from how he held me
His one year in prison was his punishment
He didn't hurt me anymore
I always tried my best to make everyone happy
I still try to please everyone
Maybe if I am kind then everyone will be kind to me
If I am good then nothing will go against me
I am trying my best

These words and memories still flooding into me
Raping me as he had done
Taking my insides and turning them to shame
Maybe I still am not doing my best?
Am I still not kind enough?
Am I still not good?

First Hospital Stay. Sometimes I Prefer to Sleep 02/01/2019

Sometimes I prefer to sleep
In my dreams the words I kept inside are said
The actions I never took happen
Scenarios of how things could have turned out play in my mind
In my dreams I fight him off; I punish him for what he had done instead of me still wondering where he is now
The thought pathetically haunting me that he could be happy in his life
Sometimes I shower with all the lights out
Only three small candles lighting my way
The darkness reminds me of sleep
My eyes closed, the candles romanticize and create stories for me
The darkness I can hide within
I can cower in the dark, let the water from the shower pour over me as I dream of the times I have felt true happiness
Sometimes I keep my headphones on, letting the music play, leaving my fan on, anything to cancel out the sounds that silence creates
In my dreams I am safe
I am brave
I sleep with my knife under my pillow
Somehow I feel safer knowing that maybe I can protect myself if someone like you came to hurt me again
Needing to feel ready in case of any random attack
I hate being another statistic
The senseless violence in overpowering someone to their weakest point and seeing the hope drain from their eyes under your hold
Sometimes I listen too hard
At work I have memorized every sound my coworkers make, I remember the usual orders and rituals my customers take

I listen to every sound around me, a pin dropping and I can tell you its exact point
I have every corner of my protected square memorized
Ready
I am ready in case someone would come after me
One of my angry customers for denying them alcohol
A robber bent on defying a corporation for every cent it is worth with no regard for the cashier's life they take in the process
I keep myself prepared
I don't stay outside too long at night
I watch for any shadow that could move
Dammit
I can't help that I like to sleep
I don't have bad dreams often
But when I do I fight back harder than I probably ever could
In my dreams I am more than myself
Sometimes I just prefer to sleep

First Hospital Stay 02/04/2019

I cradle my soul within my own broken finger tips
Light dimming as my eyes close to my own thoughts screaming
Scratching my own skin trying to readjust
My throat closed within my own heart
I shut my eyes to silence out my drowning
But I hear them fucking walking
I want to isolate but can't
I want to run but can't
I want to hurt but can't
I want to feel
But my mind won't let me

First Hospital Stay 02/06/19

I feel her eyes judging
I feel his eyes hungry
My eyes are closed

First Hospital Stay 02/06/19

I am an object in strangers eyes
Get to know me and they find me ever more appealing
I sit there steady, frozen as they touch me
At least I can make someone happy
How can you feel taken as you stood there with a smile?
I say that it is to cover up an emptiness inside
I live with my mind turned off
When it is let free it only hurts
The outward pain reminds me that I am alive
I hope to bleed to know I'm there
I hope to scar to remember myself
I sit still as I am your object again

First Hospital Stay 02/06/19

Her eyes stare judging
His look on in hunger
All I want to do is keep mine shut but no matter how tight they are I
still see his eyes looking up from my breast
What is with men and breasts?
Maybe a natural connection?
But why connect with mine?
For years I only saw Rodolfo's eyes on me, and now I see Jeff's
I see Jeff, Darrin, and Taylor
All of their eyes on me
I want to close them
I open up my feelings to trust when they only want to open my legs
I try to be kind but it feels like my cunt is all I am good for
At least when I bleed they look away

First Hospital Stay 02/07/19

I feel like I'm only as good as the dick you want me to hold
Not that I asked to look
It was pushed upon
"Look what you do to me"
"Look what you did"
I didn't do a damn thing
I sit there while you taste me with your presence
I didn't do a damn thing
Maybe it's because I don't say no, I just say I can't
I'm too terrified to say anything
You shouldn't blame yourself for others actions but shouldn't I be blamed since I technically didn't say no?
I didn't say you could touch my breasts
I didn't tell you to squeeze and feel their crevices
I didn't say you could grab my ass
Holding onto it firmly

First Hospital Stay 02/07/19

Using your crooked fingers to try to find my holes
You keep searching and all I can say is that I can't
That we will get caught
That my fiancé made me promise, that I can't
Every fucking excuse that I can
But the words NO still don't leave my lips
I am afraid to say it
Afraid of their anger
You follow me to that bathroom
Try to kiss me
Say you want to hear me as I go
I can't even escape you in my dreams
You keep fucking going
It's worse in my dreams
In them you barricade the door
The others watch us as you pull my pants off and force yourself upon me
If I don't see Rodolfo's face staring up at me I see yours
It's the same fucking hunger in your eyes
I am just an object for you to sample
I move past as you stop to take a bite
"You've got a big ass"
"How long have you had such huge tits"
Jeff says
"You kiss so well"
"Are you sure you haven't done this before"
Rodolfo says
They both ask over and over
"Does it feel good"
"Do you like that baby"

Their voices fucking repeat
I never say no
I just lay there frozen
I remember every single time I have been violated
Clear as day
My mind just can't seem to erase

First Hospital Stay 02/07/19

Most times it feels better to bleed than to feel anything at all
It's easier to make myself bleed before someone else does

First Hospital Stay 02/07/19

"You don't want to mess up your chance of going home"
The doctor says
"Honestly I don't know"
Is all I can reply
I'm afraid
I'm afraid of the unknown
What bad could possibly happen
Hurt myself before they hurt me
Hurt to feel alive
My scars are fading
I don't like that

First Hospital Stay 02/07/19

I leave tomorrow but all I can think about is how nauseous I feel
I think I'm becoming afraid of the world outside these walls
I've never been to a place like this, and I feel far from completely safe in
here
But it's not the outside
Just something about all that openness scares me so much now
It makes me feel so much more vulnerable
The patients and doctors here know so much of my story, and yet I fear
the outside world
None of that makes sense
When they ask us our triggers it can be so hard to compile a list
Most of mine stay the same but some change
1. Conflict/Violence
2. Sexually aggressive men
3. Talks of sin
4. Talking about family members dying
I'm sure I wrote down more in group but I just can't remember them all
When I leave here I worry everything will go back to normal, but I'm
not really sure I want it to
I don't know what I want
Part of me wants to go back to barely eating or throwing it all up
With my nausea I think I just might
My nerves just make me not want to eat
I go days without eating while I am here
I'm scared my family is going to want it all to go back to normal
I really don't know if it can
I'm scared
I'm scarred
I'm broken

They Never Found It

Proof that I'm broken, I still cut
They never found what I used to cut while in the hospital
They never found where I hid it
Mental hospital stay lasted from 1/29/19 – 2/8/19

Home Again

Polyamory working for us
I'm trying to be brave, but I still cut

02/19/19

I've met up with this nice guy named Andrew. We talk on and off all day. We met on a dating app. We've agreed it would only be a friend with benefits kind of deal. I'm not ready to date anyone and he is lonely since his break up with his long-term girlfriend. So far, I feel like everything is working okay. I'm talking to several people online; I am trying to take it slow as far as relationships go. I've also started talking to a guy named Mateo recently too. He's looking for a friend with benefit too.

I Get Hurt, Mateo... And Jeremy Again
03/14/9

Feeling like nothing more than a quick fuck

They always know just what to say to make a girl fall

But do they even realize that when I fall I land hard?

It's not just a crush

When I fall my soul goes with it

I crave and I get hurt

I keep feeling like I'm almost fucking there and then have my heart torn to shreds

I am told promises and look forward to them only to be slapped in the face with truths unsaid

I trust and I get hurt

These weren't the words that you told me

This isn't what you said as I laid here entangling myself in your web

You cast your spell and I was bewitched

I had begun to hope

I hope and I get hurt

For someone who has so little emotional strength, why play with my strings?

I don't think I can continue to live and love to have this happen time and fucking again

I think that I have so much love to give but my heart can't handle this strain

My mind can't handle more rejection than I already give myself

I get hurt

I am not meant to sleep around, my hearts always wants to play along

I cannot handle these feelings

All I know is that with all of these scenarios they end the same

I get hurt

03/29/19

It's strange how cold blood feels once it has left the body
I wipe away the streaks and it feels frozen to the touch
Am I so broken that even my blood cannot warm my heart?

04/01/19

I almost got caught by my support manager Ashley in the bathroom while cleaning my arm after spending my lunch hour cutting. The sink was filled with bloody water

04/04/19

I don't think I am okay. I haven't been okay in a long time. Being alone with thoughts is self-destructive. I think my mind is coming unraveled.

Suicide Attempt #3. 24hr Watch in ER 04/04/19

I was self-harming on my bed and the craving to cut deeper was too much. I'd been texting Andrew about how I was feeling. He kept telling me not to give up, that it is selfish. But is it selfish to want the pain to end? I am dying daily with these feelings. I want to blow my brains out, the voice in my head is screaming. I can't handle this. He told me to call for help so I called the suicide hot line (definitely not my first time). They said they would send a mobile crisis person to my apartment to calm me down.

Within a few minutes two cops were at my front door. I answered all covered in dried blood. They asked what I used and where it was. I told them about my blades and that they were in my room. They said we needed to wait for an ambulance. The ambulance came a moment later and wrapped my arm up after cleaning it. They told the cops I hadn't cut deep enough but that I had no choice and had to come to the emergency room for a twenty-four-hour suicide watch.

When we got the hospital, they took all of my stuff and had me change into a gown. The nurse gave me some coloring sheets because I was having anxiety attacks and she thought it would calm me down. They helped a lot. I'm so glad that nurse looked out for me all night. I stayed up too anxious to sleep. I spent the time over-thinking and listening to every sound. When I was inpatient before you couldn't really trust any of the male patients to not sexually assault you so I am listening to make sure no men come near me.

My sister was the one that picked me up in the morning. The doctor told her my vitamin d levels were nonexistent. They didn't want to adjust my meds I've been taking since I was inpatient, but did say that I should increase how much vitamin d I take daily or at least go outside once a day. The doctor begged me that I spend at least five minutes a day outside in the sun. I'm not much of an outside person anymore so we will have to see about that. Clementine (my sister) wouldn't leave me alone after taking me home. I just want to be left by myself.

04/06/19

When your arm has been burning for hours and you're not sure if it is all in your head or if it is actually sore.

04/08/19

I'm really happy at the moment, and that kind of scares me. I haven't been actually fucking happy in a very long time. Is this feeling real? Or am I just manic.

04/11/19

If someone you know struggles mentally don't tell them their self-harm scars are fake makeup. I fucking hate people.

04/17/19

Human emotions are weird. You go from being in a low head space to awesome to disassociating. I'm not sure what I'm feeling now. Can you feel everything and nothing at the same time?

04/22/19

I get asked if I am having a mental health emergency while at work, I have to lie and say no, but I am. I have to fight to keep a straight face since I am on the job. But the moment I am able to turn away I fucking break down. All night my brain has been screaming at me. I hate living. It's barely worth it anymore.

04/26/19

My brain > Hey let's wake Maeve up with a panic attack, she has only slept an hour so let's make it so that she has to buy coffee to function at work even though her heart is pounding already from 24/7 panic attacks and not eating in a week.

04/29/19

That moment when the suicide hot line employee remembers your entire conversation from the last time you called. He even asked by name how my cats were doing. I'm sure my number and info are just on some computer and they don't actually remember me. But I remembered his voice, I remembered our last talk. Something small to them meant a lot to me.

05/03/19

After having a great and public first meet up, a few dates, and constant positive communication I started dating my first partner other than Cain. He is so sweet; his name is Christian.

05/03/19

What do you do when you wake up to a panic attack that has lasted an hour now but you cannot take your old psych medications because you are trying to start take these new meds instead?

05/04/19

I am happy
I am sad
My emotions raw
To a point in my skin
Where my heart hurts of fear, confusion, and joy

05/05/19

Anxiety is completely different for everyone. It can come suddenly with no reason or days after trauma. Manifesting in nausea, a lump forming in the back of your throat. The tears form in your eye but they cannot flow for you have to keep a serious face. You have to be okay. You tell others you are fine, if they only knew how you really felt. If you told them then you know you could not hold it anymore. The exhausted wail would come out, the crying, your emotions you bottle up from others so that you don't feel like an outcast.

Your anxiety tells you that no one understands how you feel when you know that they do because they always ask if you are OKAY. Your friends know that you are not but you want to keep a strong face. You're the brave one, always there for others. The scars on your arm reminding you of your failures. They yell at you that you are not OKAY. You silence your mind by repeating your mantra. "Nothing is physically harming you. You are safe. This is all in your mind. Look at something in front of you. Remember your existence. Listen to those around you. You are OKAY. Touch the things in front of you. Your safety is real. Drink some water and calm yourself." Repeat it to yourself.

It can take time, but remind yourself that calm will come. You let your mind exaggerate the small problems large but eventually you will realize it is all OKAY. Sometimes you have to keep to yourself until the calm eventually comes. Sometimes you need the support of others. Calm will get there. Breathe in and out. You are OKAY. Remember that. You really are fine, just fine. Eventually.

05/09/19

I'm trying to be the best me I can be, but why am I even FUCKING here?

05/10/19

I was twelve years old and wearing pajamas when I was raped. Yet at the same time I was molested daily at that age no matter what I wore. I wore baggy sweats and long sleeve shirts to hide the blood and scars on my arms and yet I was sexually assaulted daily while in a hospital. Fuck the belief that an article of clothing is what really makes the difference between whether or not someone can be raped. There are court systems are out there with proof of rape yet still the victim is to blame for what they wore. Men and women can be victims. Whatever clothes they wear does not matter.

I had a fight today with some of my older coworkers, telling them that I can be naked and drunk but if someone dare lay a hand on me without my consent it is assault. Someone dare have sex with me without my consent, that is rape. Nothing else matters but consent.

05/13/19

I function on depression and coffee.

51

Christian 05/16/19

Hey. I know I say hey a lot, but to me it's been like my way of saying I love you before we ever actually said it out loud. You make me so happy; my mind doesn't even know how to form words and all that can come from my mouth is the word Hi. I care deeply for people as I become close to them. I feel my emotions with my whole body; my mind and heart passionately. I fall hard. Me telling you that I love you isn't just a simple phrase to show appreciation or admiration. Saying I love you means that I want to take care of you.

You are on my mind 24/7. I spend my days and nights thinking about plans and hopes with you. I know polyamory is new for you, I mean it still is for me. But you've been just so incredibly supportive with everything; my mental health, my relationships with friends and more, my comfort and happiness. I want to be with you forever. I want to love you and always make you feel cared for. I didn't think I could be this happy anymore. This year has been so emotionally difficult for me. There is still so much I want to tell you. It makes me so happy when you tell me we have years to continue to learn and grow together.

It's silly; when we kiss sometimes, I pull apart and just hold my forehead against yours. I'm trying to process the moment because it makes me just so happy. How is it even possible to feel this? I honestly don't even know how to respond. My heart is just so full, a smile across my face, I want to cry tears of joy just... I forgot how it felt to be happy.

05/16/20

It is weird. Being depressed and suicidal has become so second nature to me. I was going to self-harm again tonight because I am so used to it, but I didn't feel the urge to. I took a shower and I told myself I would have a good cry. But I couldn't. It's weird and it panics me a little. Pain has become second nature, is this what being happy and content with life is like?

05/19/20

I really don't know what to feel. With these medication changes I actually don't feel the urge to self-mutilate anymore. But it leaves me feeling empty now. Like what do I do? This was a release and a distraction for me. How do you just live?

05/20/20

For someone who finds themselves to be incredibly unattractive I sure do get sexually harassed on a daily basis at work.

05/25/19

So not only do I still have an over $4000 bill from when I stayed in New Haven Health for a week, but today in the mail I got a $900 bill from when I was taken by ambulance for my 24-hour watch from trying to kill myself. I live paycheck to paycheck. Even with medical insurance that I pay into monthly it's bullshit like bills that makes me feel even worse.

Suicide Attempt #4 05/31/19

My coworker/friend Jamie walked into the bathroom at work as I sat on the floor covered in blood. I was cutting deeper than I have before. My wrist, thighs, and arm were normal spots; but it just never felt like enough. There was blood everywhere. Pools on my legs and on the floor below me. She watched the door as I cleaned up. I knew with her there I couldn't keep cutting. She's so damn positive, I love her. After all of this my shift continued. Bandaged with paper towels and rubber bands, life goes on.

06/01/19

So last night my anxiety was so bad I called Cain while I was at work. I was asking him why it feels like self-harm just isn't doing it for me anymore. He says that it is because I need to fix the actual problems and not just deal with them by distracting myself with pain. Okay makes sense. He asks what the problems are and I tell him how I am just mentally exhausted, how I have things that bring me joy but I'm not happy with existing. I'm just tired of living.

He then says to me that maybe I should go back to the mental hospital, not just the ER. I gave it some serious thought. But then it's like even if I went back there all they taught me was coping skills and it was an escape from life for me while I was there just because of how structured it is. If I went back now, I don't know what I would gain. I already know the lessons they taught me. I mean there wasn't one on one therapy there; it was all about group therapies and learning to cope in healthy ways. Going back there I don't think it would honestly help with my depression at all. I know positive coping skills; I am choosing not to do them. I don't know.

I really do like my therapist a lot; she is the first one I have ever liked. I guess I want a quick fix. I want to just be fucking cured. I'm tired of fighting. I don't know. I cut because it distracts me, it can at times be a form of self-punishment. But for the most part like 90% of the time it is a distraction for me. The physical pain and focusing on what I'm doing in front of me distracts me from what I am emotionally feeling. That old poem I wrote about preferring to sleep? That's kind of how I feel a lot of the time. I mean my depression does yes make me physically tired, but also when sleeping I don't have to do anything. I don't have to work hard. I don't have to fight myself to survive. I guess at the same time I write this I am figuring it out for myself. That's another coping thing is just really thinking stuff through and writing it all out.

Second Hospital Stay 06/04/19

I checked myself back into the mental hospital I stayed at before. I'm really going to try this time. Last time self-harming starts today. Before I decided to come, I sat down with a few people, I don't know why. I guess I just needed to hear that it'll be okay eventually. Christian promised he wasn't going to go anywhere and that he just wants me to get better. That it is something I have to want for myself, but he would stay with me along the way. I talked to Jeremy after work. He told me how he is scared for me. That I am not the friend he has known for years anymore. That he loves me and just wants me happy. Jamie hugged me; she knows how it feels to have all of this emotion screaming at you. She just wants me better too.

Second Hospital Stay 06/04/19

I was placed in an all-male ward after sitting for 4-5 hours before being admitted. Admitting being the paperwork being filled out and scanned all in, being questioned on my mental status, then strip searched for contraband and to count all of my scars. They knew that I hadn't slept in 24 hours now so they placed a cot in the solitary confinement room for me to sleep some. They let me skip breakfast so I could sleep uninterrupted too.

Eventually they gave us another female patient from the other ward so that I wouldn't be the only female. Her name is Lori, she seems nice. We were given a room together after they moved one of our guys to the other ward. Overall, I have mixed feelings about the people. Like the staff are all awesome and remember me from the first time I was here. The patients I am trying to learn about to gauge how safe I feel. Memories of last time and the sexual abuse I endured from some of the patients... I don't feel safe around males, so this will be a big test for me. Lori is decent, normal lady who works on a pig farm. She deals with depression. One guy here his voice is pretty much like screaming constantly but that is his normal level of talking. He has zero control I guess to the volume, but really it seems like he just doesn't notice it. Definitely has been triggering my migraines. Another guy in a group used the phrase "shoot first, ask questions later" during a group therapy. He makes me feel uncomfortable.

Second Hospital Stay 06/05/19

Thankfully I slept well last night, it was needed with how much of a migraine I had all day. The dude with the loud voice isn't such a bad guy. Like he seems fine, just kind of never shuts up. I think he has ADHD. I know he is twenty and has a caretaker. The "shoot first" guy I found out is here because (supposedly because this is his side to the story) he had a gun out in self-defense because there were sketchy people in his neighborhood and the people called the cops on him for threatening those sketchy people. Pulling a gun for people being in your neighborhood is a very unsafe and stupid thing to do. He could've just ignored them or talked to them. I do know he has some real paranoia and PTSD from being overseas in the military.

Then there is this other guy here that talks to himself constantly. When we did a group therapy earlier, he was next to me and he literally spent the time whispering creepy shit. If he wasn't doing that then he spent the rest of the time punching and trying to pull the paintings off of the walls. He actually started the physical stuff around five or six this morning. I heard him rip a bolted painting off of the wall all the while banging the windows constantly. The only other person that is significant in my unit is this one dude. He is also quite loud. His paranoia and delusions are pretty obvious too. Like we were having a group about internal and external ways we show certain emotions. When people were saying their examples, he was yelling nonsense to himself and making his hands bent sort of like a t-Rex. You can tell he is in another world completely. The dude that rips paintings is yelling about visitation rights and government policies while raising his fists and screaming out Obama's name right now.

These people are definitely different than the patients last time I was here. Not bad, I just feel like I need to stay aware of my surroundings. Like I don't know at all what is going to happen next. The first time I was here all the patients were forced to be here by court order due to violence. Except for one girl named Marigold, she was there for self-harm like me. She was amazing. The really cool pharmacy guy that played oldies music for me to chill to last time I was here remembers me. I had to give him a urine sample earlier. He comes back up to me and said, "Maeve you're pregnant and on all of the drugs". I nearly died laughing and said how I didn't believe him for one second.

Today has been an okay day. I was annoyed plenty of times, but it was all fine eventually. I haven't felt anxious at all really, I don't think. I disassociated a few times and really needed to vomit after lunch. I did, not sure why I felt that way. Probably because this is my first time eating after not doing so the past few days. I hope Cain is okay. Me being here is just going to add another bill and empty paycheck since I am missing work. He said he was going to make healthy decisions this time while I am gone, last time I was here he nearly drunk himself into a coma daily. He skipped work that entire time and spent it drinking and playing video games. I keep thinking about Christian too. We got to talk for a few minutes on the phone yesterday. I wish so much that it could've been for longer. He was right in saying how it is such a change because we were talking all day long before. But he is also right that this will be practice for when they steal him away from me for military trainings. I can't wait until after dinner when I get to call them both. The thought still really terrifies me that Christian won't feel the same about me once I leave here. We fell hard so quickly. He says to trust him. I'm going to try my best to do so. I'm also going to have to deal with stuff with Andrew when I leave here. Before checking myself in I was texting Andrew about how emotionally raw and dead I felt. He kept inviting me over but I know it was just because he was horny and I am available. I'm wondering if Christian is right and all Andrew and I really have in common is sex. I mean we talk all of the time and like all of the same stuff but every conversation or meet up always turns sexual. I mean I am attracted to him sexually still but right before coming here how he acted on the phone. I just don't know. Him saying he didn't know if he could talk to me anymore. That hurt. I mean I guess I could stop talking to him, but I don't know. It really feels like all I am worth to him is sex. He says we are friends with benefits but it truly honestly is just benefits relationship. I want to be his friend too. Not just some fuck buddy.

Second Hospital Stay 06/06/19

Today has been fine, this new med they gave me has made me extremely sleepy though. Okay, I think I've got a few names down. Super loud uncontrollable volume guy is Justin. Loud dude that yells nonsense and does t-Rex arms is David. The one that breaks paintings and throws fits is Jacques. I still can't remember the name of the "shoot first" guy. Then there is this other guy, he gave off misogynistic vibes when we played baseball earlier. He threw the ball at me like I was a baby. His name is Brad, I do know he is here for anger and he is proud of his expansive drug use. His first day here was yesterday and fuck, you could tell he was coming down off of something. He was scary kind of angry. Claimed he had used every drug known to man on a three-day bender before being forced to come here. This young dude named Jacob isn't too bad, we talked Pokemon and Naruto a few times. Today this new guy and girl showed up. Dude has just slept in the common room all day; the girl has been crying nonstop. I know Justin is offering unwanted help to everyone. Holy shit I think David and Jacques are getting moved to the other unit. If that happens then the only bad people, I will have now is Brad and "shoot first" guy. Everyone else, even Justin, are bearable. All "shoot first" and Brad do is quietly complain. Slowly driving me nuts. This new chick is named Laurie, she is ex-Navy. Not much else there to know so far. We were told that lunch and dinner would be served in the unit today, sandwiches and pizza. Fuck, I'm sleepy again.

Second Hospital Stay 06/07/19

Today has been fine so far. Kind of feel emotionally dead though. I need to ask the pharmacist for a side effect sheet. They have me on I think two new meds now. One they said was to stop self-harming thoughts. I mean I guess it's working. I haven't thought of self-harm or suicide. But really, I haven't thought of that stuff because I'm either sleepy or emotionally dead (no feelings at all). I don't know really. I'm trying to think of positive things I want. Make a list like Christian always does. I just had a talk with my care coordinator Andy. We talked triggers, why I'm back, what I am wanting with being back. She said as long as I need help, they are always here. She said how a change in meds can be good. That maybe we just haven't found the right mix for me yet.

Second Hospital Stay 06/08/19

I get to see Christian and my mom today!!

I just saw my mom and Christian. Seeing mom was good, we had a nice honest talk. We talked about my self-harm. I burst into tears when we talked about my blades. I'm not sure I want to give them up just yet. I don't know, I think they make me feel safe. I also told her about Christian. She didn't have much to say about that other than asking if I am happy and if I still love Cain. Which the answer to both is yes. I wish I got to see Cain today but mom said he was working.

Second Hospital Stay 06/09/19

I didn't write about seeing Christian. I'm so glad I did. I don't know why I couldn't look at him. Every time I did, I just smiled way too much. Laura gave me a book she thought I would like. She has got such a cool attitude. I like her a lot. Brad I've grown to like too, he has so many questions about polyamory and thinks I am some kind of expert. There is a new girl here named Ashley, she braided my hair last night. She also came here voluntarily, but I think she is going to go back home quickly. Like maybe this was a spur of the moment decision to come here and she didn't really think it out. Bruce, the "shoot first" guy isn't so bad. I have definitely started to see a different side to him. He is a beautiful artist and does beekeeping. I think he is just one of those dad types that has a tough exterior but isn't really a bad dude. The gun thing was a bad decision though.

On the other unit I've gotten to know a girl named Petra. She is very pretty and just out there with her personality. Then there is this other girl named Bridgette, also very pretty. She is the tiniest girl I've ever seen. She told me she used to weigh over two hundred pounds. I want to look like her. She's such a positive person. Today was such an emotion filled day. In several groups we talked about people we consider family. A few times it made me tear up, just thinking of how much my loved one's support and care for me. Constantly checking up on me. I don't appreciate them enough.

Later on, we did Mr. Rays (the pharmacist I like so much) music therapy group. He let us pick a song that has meaning to us. Laura picked a Led Zeppelin song her dad played for her when she was young. Brad played "45" by Shinedown. He talked about his suicide attempt. He said how he actually pulled the trigger but it never went off. The pin didn't push the bullet through. Justin played a Linkin Park song. It hurt hearing Chester's voice knowing he lost the battle to suicide not too long ago. I grew up listening to them and even saw them in concert for my birthday when I was sixteen. Another person played "Lithium" by Nirvana. Her daughter died from her drug use and loved the band. I didn't know but found out today that Lithium was written by Kurt after a suicide attempt that failed as sort of an apology. Then he attempted suicide again but this time succeeded. Just in the time between both attempts he took the time to write the song. My song was "Ghost" by Badflower. I burst into tears describing what it meant to me. I relate to the song so much; how self-harming starts small until it continues to grow because it never feels like it is enough. I told them about all of my attempts and how I would be covered in blood but I still just didn't die. Laura and Justin comforted me. She wrapped her arms around me and told me how she understands the want to not be here anymore.

After we all were emotionally dead, they let us go outside. Sun bathing was wonderful. I just laid on the concrete and let the warmth of the sun overtake me. Today was just a lot. Emotionally draining plus feeling like I need to puke all day. It's just been something fucking else. It is the first time I have seen the sun in several days. Reminds me of my first time at this hospital. I hadn't been outside in about a week and then they took us out to a playground that the kids in the other units go to. I silently sat on the swing set that day with tears in my eyes. The blue sky was so perfect. The breeze felt like a release. Everything felt perfect and pure in that moment. Through all of the trauma I was dealing with when I was here the first time. Having multiple men follow me everywhere, commenting on my body, grabbing at me. Putting their hands under my clothes trying to get me to have sex with them between personnel checking in on us. Seeing the sun after a week of intense fear. I had never felt more at peace.

Second Hospital Stay 06/10/19

I was told I can't say I feel fine anymore. One of the techs said fine stands for Fucked up, Insecure, Neurotic, and Emotional. I'm not really sure how I feel today. Don't really feel 100% here. I feel sort of cloudy. Paul (the tech) let us sit under the gazebo. It had started to rain and I asked him if I could play in the rain, he said I could if I wanted an extra day here. So that's a no. But I did stand along the siding and held my arms out letting the water pour over me. It was beautiful. Then Paul played Beatles music for us. I felt wonderful, it was so meditative. I wish it could have lasted longer. I took off my flip flops and walked in the water as the rain let up. I really wanted to just sit in the rain while it had been pouring.

I want to hang out with my friend Jamie again when I leave here. Just hang out outside and paint like we did before after work. I've been staring at the clouds a lot and the trees surrounding the facility. I really crave painting. I'm pretty sure I am disassociating. Like I feel like I can feel my blood pulsating in my arms, back, and legs. We did a group on breathing exercises for meditation earlier. I kept trying to concentrate on my breathing but my mind kept wandering off to the pulsating feeling. I haven't heard from Cain in days. I should call Mom later to see if she has talked to him. I've left him messages. Talking to mom will help. She said a day ago that my sister had been texting him. I can't wait to talk to Christian too.

Second Hospital Stay 06/11/19

Not really sure if I am making things worse or not by being honest with Mr. Ray about my mentality. How yesterday and the day before I did have suicidal thoughts. Four people in our unit will be leaving in a day or so. Like I miss home, but I like it here too. I don't like the bill I have been adding to by staying here. But I do like the constant therapies and the friendships through trusted discussions. I don't know. We did a group based off of Robert Frost "The Road Less Traveled". Paul asked us what are some roads less traveled that we could take. I think I know what I want those three roads to be.

1. Go back to the gym
2. Finish my degree
3. Finish some of my books I've been wanting to read at home

I think these would all be good for me, at least if I actually worked on them. We have another new girl on our unit, her voice is so raspy it is driving me nuts.

Second Hospital Stay 06/12/19

We got to see Cody the therapy dog today. He was just as sweet as I remember him from last time I was here. Justin and the new chick Tammy are starting to drive me nuts/are pissing me off. Like Tammy's voice is a sick sort of raspy but every word drags on like she is falling asleep. Justin is killing me with his fake facts and saying how he knows everything. He said how he has had tons of medical issues that were all cured by eating cumin. Then he makes up these medical facts that make no sense. I think I am actually going to trip out on them. I'm not the asshole type, I try to keep quiet but part of me wants to call this dude out constantly. Like shut the fuck up bro, you don't know everything. He goes off on these rants of fucking nonsense. Plus, he chews his food and gulps his drinks so fucking loud! I've made a list of things he does over and over

1. Anything about his obsession for weed (damn well sounds like this dude hasn't smoked once in his life)
2. Saying he is "Keeping the peace"
3. His constant working out in the middle of therapy sessions to show off
4. Talking about stocks and finances when this dude has never had a job in his life

He makes it like he knows everything. I tried calling Cain earlier but got no answer. I hope he is okay. I just got Christian's letter from Andy. He is so freaking adorable. I can't wait to tell him tonight that I got it. I want to go home to see everyone but I'm just nervous that my mind will go back to where it was before. I'm nervous about feeling empty, I mean I still feel empty. But I'm nervous about feeling that way while having easy access to bad things.

Second Hospital Stay 06/14/19

Just saw Lisa (the psychologist), she says that they are thinking later next week to send me home. They are worried that sending me home now I would end up back here again. I've been here ten days now. Plus, I didn't get to talk to Christian last night. I haven't gotten to talk to Cain at all since I have been here. Missing them has started to bring down my moral. It's like I have to be in high spirits to be here and to leave but missing them makes me sad. I mean Christian and I have dated a month and now I'm gone for some time. He's going to question staying. I just know it. The only reason I can foresee Cain leaving would be because he is tired of dealing with me. I'm going to be leaving here alone. I want to cry but this medication makes me not really feel any emotions. I'm feeling sad but my body and mind aren't really reacting at all. Sheila (the lady whose daughter died from a drug overdose) is so sweet. I'm sitting in the hallway listening to Ray play "Rocket Man" and Sheila came up to me saying that I have a beautiful soul and that I have rays of beauty and love that come off of me. I can only hope that she is right. I thank her and she then says that I have left a positive impression on her.

I'm Not Really Sure 6/14/19

I'm not really sure what to feel because I've felt empty for so long now
A weight cradling my soul, holding it down
My heart heavy as I try to grasp it
My chest bare
My ribs cracked, stolen from me
I want to vomit
But there's nothing there
I'm not really sure, and I can't remember the last time I was

Second Hospital Stay 06/14/19

I still don't really know how to feel about any of this. Andy granted me permission to have an hour-long visit with Christian tomorrow. We usually only get fifteen minutes, more if you are extremely lucky on the timing and there are no groups going on. Even with this to look forward to I feel like I am going to be stuck here forever. My mood isn't going to be uplifted until I am home. I feel like I am struggling to even spell things correctly because my brain isn't working. I just want to fucking cry. I'm feeling tired and just done. It's like I felt done with life so I came here, what do you do when you feel done here? We have so many new people at the moment I can just tell that I am going to have to fight for the phone. I hate this medicine; it fixes so much but it makes me feel nothing. I just want to sleep.

Second Hospital Stay 06/15/19

I get to see Christian today. I'm going to call Mom to see if she and Cain can come visit today too. I haven't gotten to talk to Cain in so long. I want to hear his voice.

I just got off the phone with mom, she says that Cain is working all day. She said that he told her he is worried about me but wants me to stay here as long as I need. Time needs to hurry up. It is 3:17pm and my visit isn't until 5pm. I can't wait. My heart is pounding already.

Just another hour left! We are watching The Hobbit in the common room. Time needs to hurry up. We have a new guy here named Ben that looks exactly like Andrew, except no tattoos. I keep accidentally catching myself staring at him. I still haven't thought about what to do with Andrew after I leave here.

I am on top of the world after my visit.

Second Hospital Stay 06/17/19

Lisa said the treatment team will meet today about me possibly going home. It has been thirteen days. I'm anxious about going home. I don't know how to talk to Andrew again, I have to talk to my work about time needed to keep recovering before coming back. I am afraid to look at my phone when I leave here. I want to cry but I don't know. I'm just thinking about my nerves and even talking to him again. Maybe we can't stay friends. But I'd hate to lose a friend, especially one that has been with me through so much. When I was dumped by Mateo, Andrew talked me through it. I was in the middle of trying to commit suicide when he convinced me to call for help. But I'm still attracted to him and part of me feels like that isn't fair to Christian. Christian doesn't hate him, but we haven't had a good honest talk about me staying friends with benefits with Andrew. I'm just anxious and panicky about it all. It's making me shake but I can't let them know here that I'm anxious or I can't go home. I don't want to have to deal with this. If these meds didn't keep me so emotionally dead, I would be suicidal right now.

Home

Second mental hospital stay lasted from 6/4/19 – 6/18/19
I'm on eight different psych medications
I think they are working
Christian talked to me on the phone every day

06/19/19

It is my first night back from the hospital and I'm bawling my eyes out. Not bad tears, I think they are healing.

06/20/19

I had forgotten how to see a sunset
To see the colors as they cascade the sky
To feel its warmth kissing the Earth goodbye as the night comes
I had forgotten to appreciate the rain
I would dance in the summer storm
Let the drops tickle my skin
It would wash my spirit anew
I had forgotten how to feel the wind
On the swing set I felt hope
Pushing through my worries
Soaring forward like the birds I hear
I am now flying free
I had forgotten how to truly love
For my heart to ache and yearn
I craved your embrace but really I needed to feel your soul with mine
I had forgotten how to feel
I let fear rule my heart and cloud my mind
Your embrace intertwined us
Helping to calm my screams
I had forgotten how to live

06/22/19

Christian proposed today after taking me on a lovely dinner date. We dressed up all nice, drove to my apartment, and he surprised me by getting down on one knee. Then we went to the store together and picked out matching rings. I love this silly, sweet and just incredible man.

06/30/19

I don't know why but I'm incredibly anxious and nauseous. I know it'll all be fine going back to work tonight but I am panicking and crying. It would be so much easier to just give up, not go back to work. But I know I have to. Why the fuck was I born this way?

His Jealousy 07/07/19

I had trouble sleeping a few nights ago
There was such a pain in my stomach
My nerves were bundled up
Squeezing at my insides but burning my heart
The acid building in my throat wanting to escape my lips in a screaming wail
My skin feels like something is crawling
My blood boiling in a panicked rush
I feel like pain is inevitable for me
And I wish it wasn't
It brings about so much fear
Everything that has been known will change around me
I thought we had everything talked about
But maybe it wasn't planned enough
All I can say is it's too far to go back now
How things have changed since I met Christian
Just waiting now for my soul to be crushed as Cain feels I have done to his
I have fought death before but it has only continued to change its ways
Its techniques forming to what is wrong around me
Finding its way in, wanting me to give up
Things have been going so well for me
I wish they could for you
I wish that there wasn't this distance now
This silence that has grown louder, we didn't have that before
My anxiety is telling me to give in but my brain and body are too tired to care
I just want to sleep, wake up, and everything be okay
Happy and positive
Cain fine with it all

Me still able to make him happy

Us both comfortable with this newness in our lives

I wish that there wasn't that pain of rejection, of trust lost

I feel like I'm never going to gain that back with you

That it is truly gone

We want to work on us but why do we still look at each other and say nothing?

Why do you still not sleep next to me?

Why do you coil back when I kiss you?

Why does it feel like the smile you flash for just a single moment in the day feel forced?

Can we fix this? Please

I want it to all be how it was as far as us goes

But I feel like it is all a waiting game for you to leave me

The opportunity just hasn't come yet

That you are officially done with me

All our history meaning nothing

Our promises gone

You've told me before that whenever you have felt hurt that you felt there was some kind of force that pulled us back together

That you always came back

I saw it differently

I see it as every struggle we work through it together, not questioning leaving and then coming back

I've bragged about that, that we were different than every couple

That we make it through anything

Forever and fucking always

I am so scared that the light is gone

I don't feel the love in your eyes anymore

It feels like we have become strangers

Christian 07/08/19

From the moment we first met in the park you haven't left my mind
I saw you on the bench and you saw me too
But it was when you smiled
Fuck
That was the moment I started to fall
Even now I'm so in love with you and yet when I see you or hear you
speak I still get butterflies
Since I have been with you I feel like a better person
I feel happier
I am forever changed by who you are and what you mean to me
My favorite thing about you is all of you
Your love calms me
Your voice is my cure on panicked nights
Your soul is pure gold to me
And it is a privilege to be loved by you
I feel so incredibly lucky
At a point in my life when everything constantly caved in you showed
up
But you didn't save me
Instead you held my hand while I worked to save myself
When I have trouble looking at the bright side of things you come to
sit with me in the dark
I can't help how I feel around you
The way you move, it's too beautiful to look at
That's why I turn away
But I love you so much that I can't close my eyes
I know I've said this before but you help me remember how it feels to
be alive
I love you

41 Days 07/14/19

It has been forty one days since I have self-harmed and yet the cravings are still there
As if a single day hasn't even passed
That silent euphoria from the blade I felt
"Don't worry, I'm not going to kill myself"
That became a repeated phrase for me
Yesterday a friend reminded me that "Do Not Kill Yourself" was the eighth item on my To Do list
Why not the first?
Shouldn't I go through each day thinking "Yup I accomplished this, I'm still alive"
Maybe it isn't first because I'm never sure if I can accomplish that every day
Fuck do I miss the feeling
I know if I go back to cutting it will feel satisfying at first and as I go deeper the need will only intensify
Always chasing a fucking high
I miss not being okay
Maybe I'm only confusing myself
That how I feel isn't truly alive
Pain felt like meaning
Am I even living now?
I feel empty again
But I also feel nauseous

07/14/19

Of the suicidal thoughts I have had I've never imagined hanging myself. This morning after coming home from work I spent hours slipping in and out of consciousness while thinking of places I could successfully do it at my mom's house. Has my illness evolved and now I am thinking of new ways to die? I'm tired.

07/17/19

There are many things about you that I find so beautiful that it warms my heart
Your smile; I can see how genuine it is as it radiates happiness
The laughter set free, I can feel your soul
Your eyes; mixes of wild forest green, tanned sand beaches, and blue skies above
It is pure nature, your eyes shine with the colors of the Earth
Your skin; kissed by the sun all of the freckles cascading your shoulders
I love their warmth, they make me happy
Your chest strong; carrying the strength in your heart I know has been hidden within you and the years of struggles you've been through
Your hair so soft that laying against you leaves me falling into your spell
I love you
You've been through more hardship than I could find imaginable but you've kept going
God, you inspire me
You help me want to be more
To be a better version of myself so that we may grow together
I can't wait to marry you
The ultimate moment when I know our love is true
Our hearts and souls connected
Proud to be by your side forever
I love you
Everything about you
You are a dream come into reality
A love that the universe intended to come together
I hope I can be just as much for you
I love you Christian

07/20/19

I had made it forty-five days
Temptation is a sick game to play risk with

07/20/19

The past three nights I have had violent dreams. It really has my paranoia on edge.

Nightmares

07/18/19 - A demon kept taking over Jeremy's body and raping me repeatedly

07/19/19 - Cain abandons me after a big fight

07/20/19 - The store is shot up after a customer got mad and physically grabbed at me in anger. My boss Becky defended me from their attack and they decided to come back to shoot everyone in the store. A huge battle ensues.

07/27/19 - Zombies face to face with me, my mom is there. We keep killing the zombies but they repeatedly come back

07/21/19

I can feel my soul cowering into itself
The walls build around me as I sink into a ball
The shadows growing, darkening the only light I had finally found
Fuck
The oxygen is becoming sparse
It's becoming harder to breathe
I gasp for air but the weight that pushes onto my shoulders bares me down
People don't always understand how physically hard it is to be depressed
My body doesn't function the way that it should
It feels so heavy, I can barely move without my legs wanting to crumble from under me
Wanting to fall to the floor and melt into the ground
I can feel myself moving in slow motion as the world walks on by
I could reach out for help but by the time my hand gets there everyone is already gone

08/05/19

I am so tired of this life that I have. It isn't even living, I just exist. I exist doing the same fucking thing every day and get called out for it. But I can't honestly do anything to change it. I sleep, go to work, sleep again, wake up and exist for about four hours a day, then go back to sleep for work again. I get one day off a week because you can't technically count my first day off because it is spent sleeping from work, being awake for around four hours, and then go back to sleep so that the next day I can enjoy it like a normal person would with a normal schedule.

Now I get asked, why not go to day shift? I can't, you think I feel physically and mentally drained now? Day shift is worse. I have been day shift on three different occasions for a few months at a time. The crowds and the attitudes are what kill you then. So, I continue on because I actually prefer night shift. Yet I get shit on daily. My family literally every time I see or talk to them, they have to comment that they never see me anymore. I don't fucking live for myself, how do they expect me to see them when I can't even take time for myself? I used to spend more time with them, the only reason for that is because I would skip sleeping eight hours a day and would live off of coffee and energy drinks. I'm trying to make it now on one energy drink/coffee and actually getting an adequate amount of sleep.

My friends constantly ask, "What's wrong? Are you okay? Are you sure?" Yes, I am fucking sure. I always respond honestly how I feel, my life consists of the same shit just on different days. That is all it is. I keep "living" for the few people in my life that give me some sort of happiness. But I'm not alive. I'm not living. I exist to get a shitty paycheck and give it over completely to bills. So why not kill myself? Well, I've tried, and I either chicken out because of fear of hell or because I get caught doing it and am forced to stop. When the latter happens, I end up with another bill from the hospital for me to pay. Can you imagine that? I am so depressed and stressed over life, whether

I choose to ask for help myself or if it is forced upon, I end up with a ridiculous health bill. First time I asked for help and checked myself into the mental hospital in town I end up with an over $4,000 bill. I try to kill myself at home and the suicide hot line calls an ambulance for me. I appreciate that they did that, but it added a just under $2,000 bill for the 24-hour suicide watch to my stresses. Then later in the year when I check myself into the mental hospital again, I end up with another over $1,000 bill. Thankfully the most recent suicidal attempt (second time this year) my coworker/friend didn't call for help. Instead, she helped clean me up and calm me down. All of this shit is just another bill to pay.

I hate how I exist. I hate so much that is around me, But I can't change it. I can't become part time at work because I would lose my health insurance. I could go back to not sleeping but then I would be going back to drinking coffee as my only source of hydration. Go to school and get a different job, when shall I do that? Please tell me because the career I used to dream of has specific hours in which I would need to go to school for. I cannot take those classes online. I don't even know if I want that career anymore. Out of fear of the unknown, if I get that career, I would be giving up on the job I have now and know I do well at. It is a job that kills my happiness to the core, but I know I do it well.

08/06/19

We went from eight years of pet names and begging for your touch to grunts of disgust when I kiss you
To being hissed at when I reach out to touch your face
I walk to my side of the bedroom and find glass shards on the bed from the bong you threw against the wall
Didn't you think about my safety?
Didn't you care that I could've gotten hurt if I hadn't seen them and cleaned it up?
You said nothing when I asked
Come home to silence and empty liquor bottles
Drained of their substance like our relationship has
I'm not sure how I feel
I don't know if the love is there anymore
The weeks of quiet led me to prepare myself to the thought of coming home to nothing
My heart prepared itself so much, I think I fell out of love
We said forever and always
We promised
But you never told me that you would start to repulse my presence
That seeing me made you think of Christian
Seeing me and you can only imagine my partners and I fucking
Or even making love
You look at my body like it is a fungus
My growth with them has left you poisoned to the idea that we could be happy all together
Polyamory was your idea
You said this could work
It is too far gone now
I have made my marriage bed
All I asked was for you to stay by my side

But you left
Maybe not physically but emotionally you gave up and to protect your own heart you threw away mine
That electricity is gone
I don't feel anything anymore
You were my everything
But while you were protecting your heart by casting me away I kept mine safe by being ready for that
I don't know where we go from here
I keep my face forward, I still have love for you
But I will marry him
Can you handle that?
Will you stay by my side?
Will we be anything again?
Can we be anything again?
It would mean falling in love again with an eight year relationship that dwindled to nothing
I honestly don't know
I still haven't told you the wedding date
I'm not sure what I fear
My heart is ready for the bad reaction but I just don't want to experience it
I'm ready for you to lie to my face and tell me that you are fine with it when I know you are just putting on an act
Why can't you be more open like you expected me to be for you?
I can't introduce Christian to my family because they blame our broken relationship on me
Maybe I could've paid better attention to you?
But I thought I was
I apologize for my mistakes and constantly tried to move forward
But you kept fucking looking back
You blame it on me saying I am not as forward thinking as you

What does that even fucking mean?
This is all just exhausting
How can you be forward thinking when the thought process for you is
that polyamory is only fine for you to partake in
I just want positivity and love in my life, surrounding me and others
I just want it all to work out

08/06/19

I wonder if I would feel the weight sinking me down as my lungs fill up with water

If my throat would burn as I swallow the bottle of bleach

When I pour the pills down my throat will I vomit them out or drift into unconsciousness?

Would I die of a heart attack when I jump from the cliff, or will I watch myself get closer to the ground till all that is left is darkness?

Would my neck snap killing me instantly or would I dangle struggling as I cannot catch my final breathes with this rope around my neck?

Does carbon monoxide really not have a smell?

If I turn on my car in the garage, breathe in the toxic fumes, would I fall asleep gently?

Dream my final dreams until there is nothing more

I could take all of my prescribed sleeping meds, walk into the deep freezer at work, hide in the back corner behind the freight and sleep until my body cannot handle the cold

My insides frozen along with my soul

I already know how it feels to cut my own wrist, how to make myself bleed

But what if I kept going?

What if I cut deeper?

Sever the veins and nerves

Would it sting for just a moment like self-harming does now or would that pain be so intense that it is the reason I pass out?

I could drive through that intersection

While I am at the stop sign, the red light, I could slam on the gas letting the oncoming traffic hit me

They would be fine

The only one hurt would be me

These things could kill me

As I feel my thoughts have done daily
I'm in a happy place in the passenger side of the car as Christian drives
Yet my brain begs for me to open the door; roll out into traffic, letting
my body be mutilated by the cars
I want to grab the steering wheel
Everyone else I pray would be fine
Just end the pain
Stop this screaming inside my brain
I want to cry but I have to hold it all inside
I can feel the tears behind my eyes, welling up into pools
If I let it out, allowed them to fall in streams, then my screams would
erupt
My own haunting voice of guilt that causes urges within my brain when
let out only sounds like weakness and pain
It is a wail
Silent fucking screams
Grabbing my hair
Clawing my own throat
Body hunched over on my knees begging
I am begging the emptiness around me for some sort of comfort
Yelling at the Lord to save me from my own agony my mind creates
But the constant thought scares me
If and when I die what is left?
Is there an afterlife?
I believe there is but that frightens me even more, the thought that after
this life I will be meant to deal with more harm in the next
That I am meant to constantly feel this way no matter what life I am in
I feel positive moments but no true release
Fuck
I just want help
I want this all to stop
I can't even remember a life when I didn't feel this way

Why?

08/10/19

There are so many things I wish I could have seen and things I want to relive forever
Thoughts I've left unexpressed
Feelings I've left forgotten
I am scarred, made broken by my own self destruction
I can't breathe
My lungs dissipating
Grabbing hold of my own throat gasping for air
I let my eyes close as they roll back
I'm waiting to fall
But I don't
I open my eyes and stare blankly, frozen
My mind so desperately wanting to die it begs my body to just give up, but it doesn't
I'm still standing here
Just waiting for death
Waiting for this eternal peace
Waiting to no longer be in pain
I cut my wrist and watch the blood pool and drip onto the floor
I let it fall as I see it thicken and harden over my skin
For me to only open the wound again
I cut deeper this time
Instead of me tightening the grip on my skin I watch the blood flow as the lines fill with red the instant I pull the blade away
I wipe away the excess, my napkin soaked with my life's essence
Covered in desperation
The blood continues to come, I tighten my grip
Instinctively I put pressure on my wounds all the while my brain is begging itself to bleed out
Why?

I scream into the air
Please God fix me
Help me
Make this go away
Like the villain outside the victims home
Come save me
Do something to help me fight what is inside me
My heart pounds against my chest so hard that I can feel it throughout
my body pulsating
Thumping in my ears
So loud that the ringing I normally hear in silence is drowned out

08/17/19

I'm having a low night at work, and just now this cop walked past me after having bought his things. He stopped me to say, "Don't worry, it gets better in time". I know I can't hide my expression on my face but damn... okay then.

08/17/19

I want to fucking die. I'm tired. I'm just so fucking tired. My family won't accept/meet my fiancé, Christian. I'm about to lose all of my friends at my job because they all are being forced to switch to day shift since the store is cutting hours. My car is acting strange as fucking usual. I can't do shit right and it always goes fucking wrong. Why does life have to repeatedly kick my ass? All I do is my best and it is never enough. I am always doing something wrong. I'm a fuck up. Sleep is my escape but then I go through phases where I will have nightmares for weeks and then it will all go back to normal dreams. I don't have an escape. I write my feelings out but when I read my words, I feel like I sound pathetic compared to every poet I've read. I'm just venting here. I'm not going to kill myself. I'm going to bed.

08/23/19

I can feel my heart pounding
Soaring through my chest
My soul flying free
My love for you is pure magic
It has become the air I breathe

08/31/19

Christian and I got married at the courthouse today. We have decided not to tell our families just yet, have them experience our wedding at the actual ceremony this February. A few of our friends know. I haven't told Cain yet. He hasn't actually spoken to me in so long.

09/06/19 – 09/08/19

On the 6th Christian took me to Cain's work so that Cain and I could have an honest conversation. I told him the truth, about how I have felt towards him these past few months. I told him how I felt when he stopped talking to me for these past few months and how I am no longer in love with him. It broke his heart. I could see it. But he listened, and we expressed how we both feel and how we want to at least start back as friends now. If we fall back in love okay, if we just stay friends that is okay too. We need to work on being our better selves.

Then on the 8th Cain finally agreed to meet Christian. It went so well. I'm glad they finally see how much they have in common and that the three of us can work. My feelings still are confusing towards Cain, but it is known and we are finally being honest. My love for Christian grows stronger daily. He and I today (09/11/2019) actually went to look at an apartment for all three of us.

Suicidal Ideation. Attempt #5 09/23/19

It feels like the pools behind my eyes have become eternal
The dam wanting to burst
My silent screams of agony erupt as the tears flow
I have been in the cold bath water for over two hours now
Staring into the porcelain void before me
Fixated but searching for a release
My arm covered in dried blood
The coagulation thick against the washcloth as I try to clean away the
thoughts
It doesn't help anymore
The water I lay in now soiled
I turn to my side and curl into a ball
I want to drift off to sleep but it hurts knowing that my exhaustion isn't
from deaths approach but rather my own depression caving into my
soul
I want so much to be at peace finally
When can I stop hurting?
My face leaning against the wall, inches from the waters touch I cry out
Cry out to nothing
Why?
Please, fuck why?
I cannot formulate words for only guttural wails of pain come out
I can't
I don't want to keep trying
But I must
You told me about your nightmare
You finding me having gone too far
Having cut so much and too deep that I was beyond saving
I still lay in the tub as I hear your ringtone play behind me
I let it ring

Just let me give up
Let me die
Please
The thought of the horror and guilt you would feel if you found me
here
I call you back
You tell me you love me, to clean myself up, drink some water, and go
take a nap
That you'll be home soon
I'm so emotionally tired
I'm tired of trying
I'm tired of working so damn hard all of the time
How does it feel to be happy?
What is it like to not want to die all of the time?
Is it possible?
My thoughts are constantly consumed
So congested it's difficult to actually think
To think of anything other than this
Is there anything more than this?

10/05/19

Have you ever thought you were going insane?
In your own thoughts
You're alone and a maniacal laughter erupts as your own blood stains
your skin
Your friends, your spouse, your mother
All telling you that they are afraid to leave you home alone
Possibly a "danger to yourself or others" another medical chart reads
Involuntarily voluntarily committed again

Morning 10/05/19

I called my med manager after having another hard night last night at work. I don't really think anything caused it. Just that during my first 15-minute break I got curious and cut deeper than what I do on an average day. After that the thoughts of suicide just completely overtook my mind. I couldn't get it out of my head. Just the thought that I could keep cutting deeper. I texted Jamie, Jeremy, and Christian for help of even some kind of distraction. It wasn't until I got home and called my med manager that I started to feel better. She told me to call mobile crisis.

The crisis lady Nicole was really nice. We did the usual questions about my mental health. It was then that she said I had to go to the hospital. She said that I could either go with her willingly or she would have to take me in with the police department because I was considered a danger to myself at that point. Christian was with me. We went to the hospital willingly and stayed at Faith Memorial for several hours. Christian sat beside me, watching over as I laid in the hospital bed. I stayed watching the nurses and techs outside my door. Talking about taking blood tests, whispering about what I was there for. Hushed tones about what was going to happen to me. They had me get a tetanus shot, I guess they think I use dirty blades.

After a while I was told it was decided that I would be going to Kennedy Crisis Center next to the hospital. It is a shorter inpatient mental/drug rehab center. I guess in their thinking my self-harm is an addiction. I get it, but honestly since being here this place feels more like a detox center than a place to help the mentally unstable. Honestly, I just want to find a reason to live. It feels so whatever here. All that has mostly happened is we watched tv. I refused my breakfast (since I was brought in the middle of the night). I just don't care really. I know Christian visited this morning. They gave me his book and some clothes. I wish I could've seen him though. I'm not sure if this place is going to do anything for me. I'm going to give it an honest shot. But we shall see. At Faith Memorial I told them I didn't want to go back to New Haven Health because I knew I would be there for a long time. At least I had been the two times before. But at least the structure there made it feel like I was doing something. This place is just so chill. I have depression and yet they have let me sleep in my bed all day.

Evening 10/05/19

So, they honestly let me sleep and read in my room all day. New Haven Health forced you to be in group, well sort of. They at least made it so you were only allowed in your room during sleep hours, the rest of the time you were with the rest of the unit. If you wanted to sleep it was around everyone and with all of the noise. The people here said "Oh you were asleep" when I asked about Christian calling for me, or even about groups. I don't know. I ate dinner, it had been three days since I had last eaten. I also got to see Christian and my mom. I wish I was in his arms right now. He had me promise to go to the group therapies tomorrow. I guess we will see if they are pointless or not. I think I'm just going to go back to sleep.

6 AM. 10/6/19

I woke up literally twenty times in the night. I might just take my sleeping meds tonight. We shall see if today I get to talk to the psych at all. Still as always, I am feeling meh. Like I ever feel anything else.

8:30 AM. 10/06/19

It is day two here, a lady came and asked me a ton of questions about my hopes and goals. I don't know.

12 PM. 10/06/19

I just woke up to have a teleconference meeting with the psych. She seemed crazy nice. Asked me the usual basic questions. She asked me if I had ever taken lithium. I haven't so I'm really not sure what to think. But I guess we could add it to my ever-growing cocktail of medications I take. Only thing I can think of when I hear Lithium is the Nirvana song, so super not sure what to think there. The lady that interviewed me this morning also was the person that sat in on my visitation with Christian and Cain. It is so uncomfortable to have them staring and listening. At New Haven Health you only had visitation once a week for about fifteen minutes, but you got to be alone. But a positive thing here is that even though we are watched I get to see Christian everyday (for fifteen-thirty minutes).

During our visitation she told Christian and I that we couldn't have any physical contact when we were holding hands. I didn't mean to but when she said that it sent me into the lowest place. I instantly started to silently cry. My body just reacted. I hid my face from the tech but Christian I know saw my face the entire time. Cain left the room right away after she said that. I could see it angered Christian, he even asked the tech if we could set up an appointment and meet at a time when she wasn't there. Any other tech but her. She got super defensive. It made me just freeze up; confrontation makes me uncomfortable. When he left, I was stuck in that low place still.

I'm back in my room and I hear the tech now talking about me to everyone. Angry and defensive about the rules, but I get it. They don't want drugs to be passed along at visitations, even though I am not here for drug use at all. Plus, we are searched after every visitation. I want to self-harm and honestly just fucking die. I'm tired. I saved a plastic piece from breakfast to self-harm with. It takes forever to actually cut with it though since I have become accustomed this year to using razor blades. Although when I was nineteen when I would cut, I was very used to using household objects. It's frustrating. The techs questioned me a bunch about Cain visiting. I kept telling them that he is allowed to visit, even though he is my ex we are still friends and roommates all three of us. The techs claim that I said I was uncomfortable with him being around. Pulling words out of their ass, making stuff up. I don't know, I'm going to go back to bed.

1 PM. 10/6/19

I wasn't allowed a fork at lunch just now. I heard the tech and the pharmacist talking about it. I guess that means I am on suicide watch. Not surprising though, told them this morning that I wanted to. I have a migraine. I wish I had my razor blades. It just relaxes me knowing I have them close. I feel bad for Christian. I just got off the phone with him and he is so confused. Just completely backwards. I handle the bills and organizing so he is confused and keeps losing things. I wish I could help him, sweet man.

7 PM. 10/6/19

I don't like the way this old guy that is a new patient was staring at me. I have to keep my eye out for him. We just had dinner and I still have a migraine. They gave me some pain meds. Earlier today they asked me if I have/am hallucinating. I don't know if I am or not. Stuff feels like it is going slower than it actually is. Think like the timeline that followed people in the film Donnie Darko. I haven't told them though. It doesn't concern me much. It feels like my normal disassociating but with some extra to it. I slept all day today which means I'll be up all night again.

8 AM. 10/7/19

Last night was something else. I woke up to someone giving me my meds. She tried to give me a few meds I didn't recognize, refused me my birth control, and then claimed my meds that I normally take were never ordered. I told her how my medication list I brought in is opposite, AM. means PM. since I am a night shift employee. She wouldn't believe me and kept speaking to me in an accusatory manner. It's not like I was asking for narcotics. I just want to take my blood pressure, anxiety, and birth control meds at the correct times so that I don't mix up my schedule or accidentally double up on something.

So, like every time when I get angry or emotional, I instantly started crying involuntarily. She stormed out of the room and started shouting to the techs how I was being demanding and refusing to take my meds. She came back into the room and asked if I wanted to "skip all of the meds, take some Trazadone (my sleeping pills), and think about taking my correct meds in the morning". This made me cry out that I wanted to go home and talk to my husband. She stormed off again. So, I went to the bathroom and locked the door behind me as I sat on the floor crying and scratching at my wrist. I used the hidden plastic piece that I have to cut along my wrist. The bad part about using plastic is that you have to continuously do it for anything to actually happen. It isn't as easy to harm yourself with. The nice tech I talked with once knocked on the door and we sat on the floor and talked. Eventually I left the bathroom but stayed awake paranoid in my room. The supervisor came in and told me I would be getting all of my meds and not to worry. When I went to see the med nurse again, she still refused me my birth control but allowed me to take my normal meds for bedtime. The nice tech came and checked on me, I told her how I was still refused my birth control. After a little back and forth I finally was able to get all of my meds, swallowing them dry. I didn't trust the water she tried to give me. I ended up staying up half of the night. I just want to leave here. I'll be stuck seeing that nurse again tonight while all today I am stuck with that fake nice lady that was rude to Christian and I. I just want to be home.

6 PM. 10/7/19

Today hasn't been a bad day at all. I think it is because there has actually been a decent group of techs. I've overheard them talking about me leaving tomorrow at 12 PM. My visit with Christian went well. The tech in the room made it comfortable, not like every other tech that feels like they are watching and judging. I feel okay other than the migraine and disassociation. All the disassociating is starting to bother me. But I guess I just have to deal.

10/08/19

I finally am home. Christian came to pick me up from Kennedy Crisis Center. His boss let him have the day off so he could spend it with me. They've surprisingly been really understanding about all of this, texting and calling him to give them updates on how I am doing. He greeted me at the gate with flowers. My heart warmed up instantly when I was in his embrace again. I've missed being held by him. I've missed how comfortable and safe he makes me feel.

Nightmares 10/19/19

I've felt fine for days now
Only to wake up drenched in sweat
My dreams so vivid my body reacts as if it had really happened
My heart pounding, I feel flush
My soul panics
I look at my spouse lying beside me and he feels foreign to me
He sees me looking and I tell him of my nightmares
His hands reach out to hold me, comfort me however he can
But I feel wrong within my own skin
A tingling sensation along my spine
My hair raised
Fear
In my dream I remember I felt so afraid of everything
I didn't want to be touched, I was desperate
I was constantly screaming in terror and pain
To make it worse in my dreams I was made an object repeatedly
The bile in the back of my throat a reminder
I already have to deal with enough anxiety in real life, why do my dreams always turn into nightmares?
The images replaying themselves for hours throughout the night
Any time I fall back asleep it starts again
Where can I escape to if even in sleep I cannot hide?
I cannot be happy

We Both Worry 10/22/19

You worry about me
I can see it in your soul, reflecting through your eyes
I know when you leave for work you wonder what you will come home to
You spend your days messaging me when internet is available just to have some sort of communication
Needing to know I am still there
On my bad days you tell me to go hang out with my mom
To go see my friends
You give me a to-do list
Anything you can to keep me busy and focused on anything but my thoughts
You've told me before that you're afraid to leave me alone sometimes
I worry about you
Even when you don't say it I know
I see the way you look at me
So in love but desperate to save me
When I'm in the bath alone for hours cutting you stand outside the door begging
I can hear you trying to break through the lock
I tell you through tear stained cheeks that I don't want you to see me this way
You reply that you already know, that you just want to be there for me
Please
You don't know
You can imagine, but I can't let you have that image of me in your head
I can't let you remember me that way
I clean off and let you in
You stand there protective, watching as I clothe myself
Hiding the scars I know you've already seen

Trying to keep you safe from my pain
You have your own depression to deal with
I ask you, do I make your own mind worse?
You say nothing
We both know
You tell me I don't
But I know I cause you pain
I know that you wouldn't be afraid all of the time if I was actually happy
You tell me you love me
Hugging me tight I feel the tears fall from your eyes onto my shoulder
You tell me that all you need is me
That I make you happy
That I make it all better
Then you whisper in your embrace as I've heard you say before, "Please don't leave me"
You never have to fear of a divorce, but we both know what you mean
Don't let my pain become so much that I cannot handle it anymore
I wipe your tears
I kiss your nose
How could I do this to someone so sweet?
I can save you from your depths but aren't my struggles part of what bring you there?
Fuck
The way you grew up and have been treated in life
You deserve better than me
You deserve everything wonderful and happy
But at the same time I know I need you
Through all of the bullshit I feel daily you make me want to live
Seeing you
Seeing your face, to hold and to be held by you
You comfort me

10/25/19

I don't know if I know how to be okay
When I'm alone or unoccupied you would think my mind can relax
and be at ease but all I can really focus on is the "what's wrong" or the
"how can I feel depressed today"
Then I start to over think and wonder if I want to be okay
It's not like this is some kind of an attention grab, actually I prefer to
isolate when things get bad
But, I feel like I only know how to be in pain
Like everything is a fucking struggle of whether I want to live or die
Whether I want to exist or hide away
I find comfort in my hiding and being alone
But won't I eventually become lonely?
Part of me sits here and thinks about how good I will feel leaving my
job and my friends behind
I wouldn't have to put forth any energy
I can just sit at home
Stay at home
Just stay with my husband and my cat
Cancel everyone out
But do I really want that?
Would that make me happy or would it make things worse?

10/31/19

I go back to work tonight. I'm anxious, but also okay. I don't know really. I guess all at the same time I don't really feel anything.

11/03/19

My med manager and I agreed that it would probably be best if I shorten my work week. Instead of working full time I will become barely even part time. It will mean more stress because of less income for our household, but hopefully it will lower my anxiety being able to relax at home more. I'm not really sure. I guess everything is worth a shot.

A few days ago, I met with my med manager to talk about my medications. We stopped me from taking my self-harm meds (obvious it isn't doing anything for me). Now I am starting Latuda to take along with my other meds. So far, I feel pretty much the same emotionally, just meh. But this med definitely knocks me out. My self-harm is pretty much the same. I mean it isn't as bad as the beginning of this year when I would spend hours every day cutting, but I still do spend my breaks and lunch at work doing it. Plus, once in a while for a few minutes at home. It is just a relief sort of feeling now.

I've gone through phases where it helped me to remind myself that I was alive, then for it to be sort of a punishment type feeling, all the way for it to become a way to shut off the thoughts in my head. Now it has become like a cigarette or alcohol for "normal" people. Just a sigh of relief. I'm still careful and always clean myself up. But I do cut slightly deeper than I used to.

11/04/19

So yesterday night at work Jeremy came up to me and said that he needed to tell me some news. I sort of sat there and guessed he was going to tell me that he was no longer single (even though he has said he doesn't want a relationship right now since he and his wife broke up). I mean I am happy he is out there and trying to find his happiness but part of me is upset I never even got a chance with him. Yeah, I kind of just wrote a bunch to myself fighting with how I am feeling.

I'm not really sure how to feel

Part of me wants to be mad

I wasn't even given a chance

Egotistical me, thinking that having one date would have been enough to make you want me

That's fucking pathetic

Am I so desperate for attention?

Part of me feels nothing

After a year of practically yet pathetically begging Cain for a shot with you I knew it was coming so why be upset?

Part of me is jealous

I don't even know why

I mean Christian is the greatest guy to come home to daily but I fought hard for so fucking long to even get one fucking chance

What do I want here?

It's done

It's over

Get over it

I think I'm having trouble getting over it because it had become such a big part of my life for a time period

All Cain and I could do was fight over it

But I mean so much has happened since then

I don't know

Then you go and tiptoe around it worried that telling me any truths
would make me go and kill myself
I get it
I don't handle stress well, but I'm not fucking glass
Everything about me doesn't just break
Part of me, for a while actually, has been telling myself to distance away
from everyone
My wedding invitations still sit in a bag in the car
I'm just tired of caring or trying
It's exhausting
I prefer to sleep
I wake up to the sound of my husband's voice
He is all I need
I've been separating myself slowly from friends
Less messages, less eye contact
But I doubt this will bring me any happiness
It will probably just make things worse for myself
I'm destroying the people who care about me
I spent the beginning of this year tearing myself away from my family
to make the thought of killing myself easier
It worked sort of
I mean my love for them all changed
Being afraid to die out of fear of hurting my family went away
But they guilt me constantly about separating myself
Now for the past couple of months I've been repairing what was lost
and you would think I'm happy
Yet I want to do it again but this time with friends
I want to stop talking to them all
The effort is just exhausting
This is only going to make things worse for me
I know it
I don't know what I'm doing

Am I finally happy and my mind is fighting itself trying to destroy it
just so I can go back to struggling again?
Is this my suicidal ideation creeping by sneaking around and distancing
myself again?
I don't know
I guess I'll just keep my head down like always
Just stare at the floor and keep going day by day
I don't know

10/22/19 – 11/05/19

On the 22nd Christian took my computer and wrote a small poem for me. He said that I needed to write a happy poem for him by the end of the day. It was his way of helping me cope that day. Thing is, I didn't write it until the middle of the night last night. I just haven't felt inspired to write.

To me you are everything
Without you, I am nothing
My mind without you in it is an absence of mind
I love you Maeve
- Christian
My response
Smile forms across my face
Being held in your arms
My lips against your skin
I breathe in your scent
Sweet English black tea
Your soul is free
I could see you caged for so long
I'm so in love with who you are and what we can be
The gentlest eyes I've ever known
Falling into their gaze my fondness for you grows
My heart swells with the admiration you show
The safety I feel with you
Protection I have for you
It's a beautiful comfort
It's the close your eyes and fall back trusting kind of love
It's that give it all my heart and soul I bind myself to you kind of love
You're my everything Christian
You're all I've ever needed

You're everything

Now When I See You 11/16/19

Jealousy is the bitter fruit that burns my cut lips
Scarred from nervous laughs and wishes
The beautiful lake of hope I walked on was only a mask for the shattered glass that cuts me now as my heart still wants to step upon
The thick pill I have swallowed down in gulps as I suck back in the tears
Look at me
Sitting here my mind coming up with more and more ways to compare how I feel
It's all just bullshit
I sound pathetic
I don't even know if I'm jealous or just damn angry
Both?
I don't know, maybe I'm looking for an excuse to feel something but to me it just sounds obsessive
I'm fucking pathetic
I look at you and there is some sort of resentment
Why?
You didn't do anything wrong, you weren't cruel
But as fucking always I fell too hard and over thought everything making it more than it was

11/16/19

I taste the metallic blood from biting down on my lip to hide my outcry
I wipe away the tear as it starts to fall so that your hand won't catch it
as you wrap your arms around me
For years masturbation was how I reminded myself I was alive
It was how I found any pleasure in living
You always wonder how I can be horny all of the time
But I'm not sure that I am
It makes me feel good
It brings me some sort of happiness in my constant depression
But lately every time we make love all I can do is have flashbacks to my
rape and abuse
Not that it was violent, it wasn't
But the feelings of lying there being taken
You're doing nothing wrong
It's just my own fucked up head
Turning something beautiful into another fucked up part of me
Your cum, what would give me pleasure and warmth feels like a burning
sting now
My body is reacting to it in repulse
But I don't mean it
Fuck, I promise you're doing nothing wrong
It's me
It's always fucking me
My brain can't have anything anymore
Last time we made love and when I left the room to clean off I cut my
wrist to shut off my brain
Right now my body is begging itself to self-harm but I don't want
you to wonder when I come back into the room why I cut right after
expressing our love

The positive part about you having me bent over is at least you can't see my face

You can't see the anguish and pain that I know my face cannot always hide

What is wrong with me?

When I go back into the room I'm going to have to fake a smile like everything is fine when really I am screaming inside

My body is shaking

My nerves bundled and electric wanting me to run away from my problems

But where dammit?

Where do I run to?

Do I go back to how it was before when I would drive off on my own to cut for hours to relieve my tensions?

I can't do that anymore

I can't make myself worse again

I can't make you question and wonder

Worried about me

I'm sitting in the damn bathroom wondering what to do

I'll go back to the room and try my best to hide my face as I fall back asleep beside you

Why does my mind always have to attack itself?

Can I have nothing good in this world?

I can feel the tears behind my eyes but I have to push them back in

Smile like nothing is wrong

You're fine

There is nothing physically harming you

This is just your mind fighting itself

You're going to be okay

11/16/19

Sometimes I sit and think over and over that I'm done
That I've had enough of this world
To please just pull this plug
It's sad
I have a screenshot saved in my phone of a news article about this girl
She had decided to tell her family that she had talked to doctors about assisted suicide
That she had spent years thinking about killing herself, even had attempted it several times
But she was finally done
I don't know why I have had that picture saved for months now
There are many times I sit here and think about how I just don't care about anything at all
Or is it caring too much that it feels like everything?
I don't know
How long will I be writing these thoughts out?
It helps
It helps me to better understand myself, to think completely
My pain is expressed through my words
But I don't want to feel this pain anymore
I don't want to be anything anymore
I am a prisoner to my own thoughts
I have created Hell in my mind
I've had enough with living with the ghosts of my past
Of my innocence being taken
All I do is dream repeatedly of hate and pain
Yet when I am awake I dream to kill myself
It's constant

11/17/19

I'm waiting for you to fall out of love with me
It all happened so quickly
I know the infatuation will end just as fast
You love me now
But why?
I'm a depressive fuck that is in a constant low state
I bring you down
A constant suicidal tendency that's just another hospitalization from you running away
You have your reasons to leave me
It's all justified
I'm fucking nuts
She's crazy
All she wants in life is to die
It's unhealthy
She's sick
I'm just waiting
I'm meant to be alone
I'm meant to be left to die
There's nothing good about me or worth saving
There's nothing worth living for

11/21/19

So, a few days ago I talked with my med manager Ashleigh about my low weekend. How bad the thoughts were in the forefront of my mind. We thought that making it so I take my Latuda twice a day instead of just once would help with alleviating the tiredness that stresses me out but also making sure I get enough med to help with the depression. The next day I met with my primary care doc to talk to her about how I am always dizzy and I'm not sure if it is my anxiety or what. She thinks I am taking too strong of a blood pressure medicine, so we stopped it. It makes sense that it is too strong even though I have been taking it for years. With my anxiety I have lost over 40 lbs. this year from starvation alone. I'm better now about eating every day at least though.

But back to the meds, since I have stopped taking them the dizziness has gone away. These past few days have been good. I am keeping myself busy and finally my anxiety isn't so high that I am constantly shaking and having panic attacks. I was like a scared chihuahua all weekend with the nervous shakes. I also haven't self-harmed in four days. I can't promise that this is some sort of permanent change with me. But I am

trying really damn hard. I don't see my therapist again until the 5th of December so I need to try to keep this good going.

Christian was so supportive during this bad weekend. I know we were trying to go to sleep Friday night but I was shaking so bad just panicking. I told him how I was wanting to go to New Haven Health but I didn't want to be away from him. You only get to have visits for maybe one hour (usually fifteen minutes) once a week. Phone usage is hard to handle too trying to use it when everyone wants to as well. He held me as tight as he could even after I finally fell asleep. It is always weird when I have good days, it just isn't common for me so I don't know how to feel or react. But I am trying not to just sit around thinking, doing that I start focusing on the bad and then I start to feel bad. Then it all just spirals back into the negative.

11/30/19

On the 17th of this month was the last day I self-harmed. That weekend was incredibly difficult for me. One of the ones out of many I won't be forgetting any time soon. I called out of work each day even. My anxiety and the shaking were just too bad. It would've freaked out my coworkers and customers if they saw me. Shaking like I was coming down off of something. When really, I just couldn't calm down. My depression was just too bad. Suicide was at the forefront of my mind and I couldn't get it to go away. Damn, imagine if I had gone to work. I might not be here right now. It isn't a myth that at work I don't make the best health decisions when it comes to cutting. My job was the place where I've done the most self-harming. Also, the location of one of my suicide attempts.

That weekend on Friday night with Christian I remember just lying-in bed crying. He held me as I was shaking. Held me tighter than ever before as I sobbed. I wanted to die so much in that moment. I told him how I honestly wanted to go to the hospital but I knew I couldn't handle not seeing him daily. I told my med manager the next day honestly how every day death is the only thing on my mind, but I know even with these thoughts I don't really want to die. I'm just desperate to be better. Christian asked me that day to try at least for one day try not to cut. I've been taking this one day at a time. The urges are gone. This doesn't feel like last time when I stopped. Before, the cutting stopped but the urges stayed. I thought about it constantly. Now I only think about it sometimes. I think about the feelings of relief it gave me. I think about the little things; the way I focused on the blade, how I became mesmerized with the blood as I watched it fall. Okay, I should stop now.

The actual urge to do it isn't there, my mind just likes to wander and as my therapist calls it "self-sabotage". I still haven't gotten rid of any of my hidden blades around the house. I don't know if I want too just yet. But maybe this is a good mix of meds for me. I've been feeling okay. A lot has happened too since I have stopped cutting. I quit my job and signed up for school in January. I'm going to try to finish my degree I stopped working on when my depression had gotten bad when I was nineteen. Thirteen days of no self-harming. I spend my days at home trying to find my peace. I'm extremely lucky to have Christian. He is so incredibly supportive of me. Always taking care and making sure I have no worries except getting better. I've started painting again. It isn't a daily thing but it makes me smile and keeps my mind busy. My therapist told me to try to do things throughout the day to keep my mind busy and not so that it wanders to negative thoughts. I'm trying, and it feels like succeeding for once.

12/17/19

Everything has been going okay. I mean I guess I just keep focusing so much on the past when I just sit and think. My days are spent relaxing for the most part. I clean the house, paint, watch TV. Next month I start school. I've been the best I've been this entire year. I don't mean to think back on the negative. I guess I'm just getting myself ready for when something will go wrong. I still have not self-harmed. I'm proud of that. The urge isn't there. But the memories are clear as day. I look at my arm and see the scars fading. It's as if they aren't there almost anymore. Part of me misses them. They were part of me. They were mine. But they are fading now. I miss them. I miss it. I would keep myself clean and bandage myself up. It was mine to keep and care for. God, I sound demented. I still have all my blades. I don't want to get rid of them. I haven't touched them in weeks. It feels like it would be foreign at the same time. Like an old friend you haven't seen in forever but have such a history it's like no time has passed.

I sound awful. I should be proud. I've come so far. But the memories of all the struggles, of all the days and nights I fought so damn hard. Then there are memories of the hospitals. I want the memories of the bad to go away but at the same time I don't want to forget everything. I think I'm just scared it all could happen all over again. That something will fuck up or stress me out and it will all just unravel again. Every time I cut; I was just inching myself closer to death. It was always me wanting to kill off what I was feeling even if it meant my actual death. Now I'm doing better, but am I really? Always self-sabotaging in some way. I am doing better. I shouldn't worry so much. Things are going well and will continue to go well.

I see my therapist every Thursday now. We've been focusing a lot on mindfulness. I remember barely learning it in New Haven Health. At least what I did learn I wasn't successful at it. I get it. I guess I'm just not in the mood to meditate so I've been annoyed with going. My therapist is great. I'm just being a grump. I feel like I want to work on getting over my past, but is me not keeping myself focused on my past meaning I am better now from my thoughts? None of that made sense what I just said. I don't know. Forget it. I just feel like there is still stuff holding me back and I don't know what parts of me it specifically is but I just want to vent and feel but feel good. I don't want to keep feeling like I am existing, I want to feel like I am living. I want to feel at peace and positive and just one with everything. I feel like a floor mat. I'm here. Stuff is happening and I am part of it. I interact with what is around me but that is about it. I don't know. I ask for too much.

12/27/19

Just let me go
Just let me die
What part of me is worth saving?
For the longest time I've thought that I lost part of my soul and that
still reigns true
I don't care
But I also care so much that it feels pointless
I have no passion for anything
I exist
Everything, being, it's just a lot to handle
I don't write anymore
Painting feels unworthy
I hate how I look and feel
Everything feels too much and not enough to matter
Just deal with me till I die off
You don't have to love me as sweetly as you do
Let me exist in this
I don't need anything
I won't ask for much
I can go without food
Without conversation
Without notice
Just let me lie here existing until I fall off into nothing